From a Sandstone Ledge

poems by

Shelley Armitage

Finishing Line Press
Georgetown, Kentucky

From a Sandstone Ledge

ACKNOWLEDGMENTS

Llano Estacado, Intaglio, and Memory in Water, *Texas Poetry Assignment*
I'm As Old as Turtles, *Senior Class*

Publisher: Leah Huete de Maines
Editor: Christen Kincaid
Cover Art: Shelley Armitage
Author Photo: Greg Conn
Cover Design: Elizabeth Maines McCleavy

Order online: www.finishinglinepress.com
also available on amazon.com

Author inquiries and mail orders:
Finishing Line Press
PO Box 1626
Georgetown, Kentucky 40324
USA

Contents

For Deborah
For those who, like Leslie Marmon Silko, believe
"we are nothing without the stories"

Llano Estacado

Flat say the tourists shaming the 75-mph speed limit with their blur/
                    I-40, I-20, I-27

Featureless, the explorers wrote disappointedly, *the Great American
    Desert, a sea of grass/*
                    from the Canadian River to the Edward's Plateau

Called the *staked plains* in folklore, ancients were said to mark
        a
                    route with
                            pilesofstonebone

        and even cow manure—guides through the rudderless land

But who could trust such markers if made by the likes of Coronado's
Esteban   meandering toward   what he claimed
    were the Seven

                    Cities of Cibola, with only dusty pueblos waiting.

Truth: the flatness is a gradually
                            tableland
                    tilting

One
        of the largest plateaus in North America (37,500 square
miles). Any person on horsebackorwalkingwithanoticingeye
can
        feel   lift
                    that slight

the plateau appears atop

From below   stockaded
                                palisades
                              reaching to
                                the caprock
                    thus   so named:
                    llano estacado.

Featureless? Creosote cholla gramma mesquite prickly pear
juniper and trust the pronghorn, themselves v
          er
                    tical, to sniff out forbs bladderwort Mexican
buckeye acacia ironweed vervain daisies verbena crown
beard purslane panhandle grape vetch deer pea violet
mustang grape goldeneye not to mention bear grass, yucca,
pondweed much more   like watery

          P   s
            l   a
                    a   y
                    too,   life sustaining   shimmering
                    silver dollars   where there is no gold

who would not want to be defined by an endless
          horizontal yellow like this
                    often bluing into purple, mornings, evenings
                    as if looking over the cusp of the
                              world from a sandstone ledge
                              no matter how lost

Intaglio

Drought knows no boundaries
kochia weed and creosote hug both sides
what was—long ago—a photo op sign
now is a drive-by
NJ, IN, NM, OK, ILL, HI, AK, and more
bumper to bumper on this highway
connecting coast to coast.
Once a lark, its predecessor, Route 66, passed through Glenrio
here
no glen, no river, straddling the NM/TX state lines.
The town had a bar and Little Juarez, a café,
a gas station on one side
(no state tax), a bar on the other,
(a wet county) —drought excepted.
Daddy, daddy, we begged, *get the camera*
Daddy, daddy, stop please!
Stair-steps, those photos, like the monument's
rock foundation, weathering faded years, now gone.
We'd climbed aboard, embraced the granite icon
graced its stately shape with our odalisques
unaware that any Comanche had passed by
collecting plants for medicine bundles
their weapons striking the speaking rock
now replaced in forgettable vinyl green:
Welcome to Texas, *Drive Friendly*
The Texas Way.

Memory in Water

"The wild God of the world is sometimes merciful"
—Robinson Jeffers

It's what he has: black bottomed plastic,
algae corners, slow evaporation of
      what is already wastewater.

Thrawn tumbleweeds accumulate, gnats swarm,
but really there's nothing to eat.

Workers from the domestic water association
manage the treatment plant. They float above him—
      conjunto music, and wind trimmed talk—
then grind out the connecting road in ATV rattles.
      Nonplussed, he strokes the water.

It's been nine weeks now and no flight.
On morning walks, I peer through the chain linked
      fence that jails the ponds. DANGER
Chemicals on Site. A hefty chain and lock
discourage trespassers. What to do but watch
      and wait. When I phone, the company operator
assures *they sometimes take him food.*

He suns (there's no shade), paddles, makes
his way in circles, his flock already gone for the summer.
      Might he be like your hawks, Robinson,
hurt and grounded but without their pride that
earned a leaden end?

      He's a Ring-Necked duck, un-
assuming in his indigo necklace, his body
a muddied flash of white against the slime,
      and that other white—a tiny bright wrap around

his dark beak. His breeds' distinction? The instant
take-off, no labored flapping, no scattering on the
            wet runway. Top speed, 60 mph.
That's how strong his wings should be.

This morning he sits along the pitched wall of the pond
at water's edge. For some reason he can't fly
            and he can't walk out.
Perhaps it's the reflection of sky in the water
that makes him think he's still flying.

Yesterday I glimpsed a female beside him.
Side by side, they fluffed their feathers.
            I watched to see if she would follow him in his
methodical foray. She didn't. She flew away.
He was left again with occasional visitors—but not
            to him—to the water: quail, thrasher, killdeer.

What I know about ducks comes from a feed store,
Easter time, we kids begged for one of the ducklings.
We filled our plastic kids' pool, put out some grain,
            while waiting for next day's Resurrection.
That morning our duckling lay lifeless, an upside-down
yellow in the blue pool, some miraculous balance
tipping his feet to the sky. Crying brought no wisdom,
no realization except that of the first raw feeling of being alone.

We're companioned are we not, you and I,
by my daily visits. My aloneness meets yours.
Yet I am less alone when you are here
and to be here you are less free.

Texas Spring During Covid

In this moment you have changed
Bishop's cap a mouth, unspeaking,

sipping air, ignorant of neighbors
slamming doors, motorcycles like a pack

of wasps, the fart of an old truck.
We are told *shelter in place*, yet

people rush as the wind picks up
before dusk carrying vibrations

of a border helicopter slicing air.
You stand, slightly swaying

a leaf of peace.

This is your ripening time
and I am drawn to get the hose

bring water—a small penance
to you, the saint, who, green and patient

all winter, restores calm,
a creative waiting

One iris is blooming; the world is on fire.
Can we remember the rhizome faith

when bloom is done, when we
are left with only spent stalks?

You are not perfect. You bend
with less than a full head

in this Texas wind. But beauty
seems even greater when shaped

by harbor and stealth, by fear and trembling.
Will your bloom be that old-fashioned purple

or one of the flashy new varieties? You are
cousin to those irises of old, stubborn still

tubers of time, of memory of sun,
and moisture and stillness.

I unfurl the hose, bring the holy water:
you tap an inner sweetness

in this supplicant turned steward,
in this gesture of love.

Xylem and Phloem

Where did you come from, circling
pow-wow style, in this old farmhouse

huddled like women at a bridge game
No *bye baby bunting   daddy's gone a hunting*

No *rockabye baby in the treetop.*
Only silence in motion.

One of you, the most elegant, polished
back like a swan's display

witnessed the loss of my stubborn virginity
(you were in the front room, but you saw, you saw)

Another, the death of the oldest settler
in Oldham County (your mission style hand honed, reserved)

And another where my grandad's extended leg
(later lost to diabetes) bounced this baby on his

arched foot: *Pony Boy   Pony Boy*
Won't you be my Pony Boy

Don't say know   here we go
Riding 'cross the plains

I liked the giddy-up part the best.

The third holds an old friend's gift
a small white teddy bear she made

from an old nubby Chenille bedspread
(whose, I wonder?) dimpled arms akimbo

The smallest of you belonged
to my great-great grandmother

fit for women, generous seat, dainty legs
Here she trimmed her quilts until age 102

You gather together—a group of hand-me downs,
a council of elders

I sit on the platform one, my grandfather's
careful of its stiffening springs

I stroke the wooden arms smoothed by grasping
and realize this is not child's play:

Old Rocking Chair's Got Me.

Four rockers, each its own story—
maple   walnut   cedar   ash—

once the heart of forests   now the seat
of our joys and fears and careless days.

Trove

The treasure lay at the foot of the bed
but my small pirate mind could only dream
of cowgirl outfits and loyal horses those lazy
summer afternoons, napping on my parents' bed
beneath a sonorous evaporative cooler.
All these summers later—over seventy as a matter
of fact—I still can sleep to the sound of coolers.
But this old farmhouse awakens me with its quaking,
each footfall a resonance now that the cedar chest has
almost outlived us all. Was it a wedding gift, this yawning trove—
hefty flat top, rounded legs precisely lathed—hues of tree flesh
filled through the years by my mother, spicey smell still
filling the house with promises of preservation
and *do not touch*. I cautiously open the lid
expecting something living to jump out.
Instead there are dead things we call memories, pressed,
trapped sediment—layers of Roy and Shelley photos
(baby's first year and beyond), of Mother's Day cards
mixed in with Roy's horticultural project, yellowed photos
of collected roots dangling, and my cowgirl skirt,
his report cards (really? all those A's?), that pink plastic
bobbing cradle toy (I do remember), a riffled envelope with
my cousin's baby pictures from Poznan Poland where she was born.

More photos too, Pat, Joe, Mark, the other adopted kids in town.
I stop at the letter, laminated, from *The Texas Children's Home
and Aid Society*, to save something of mother's touch
for later. Thinking of the tiny tarantula I found earlier
hiding within the backdoor facing, a dot of difference
to be eradicated (who knew what it was, not to spray?),
one newborn among thousands, now a castaway trailing
black liquid, I wonder at what mother had chosen to save:
whose story, whose sting—in this tangled wilderness
I call home.

Big Brother

Like a clock wound tight clicking forward to return again, he
counted the white blood cells over and over, day by day/ in
each long distance phone call I made meant as a distraction
they echoed in his voice a feigned devil may care against
the tick, tick, tick, the drip, drip, drip/ Footfalls vibrated
too, in those stories told above ground reverberating in ears
flattened like walls/ I was blue with breath held tight chest
pounding in this post hole he's put me in—gently, a joke,
my destiny—he then rescued me from/ Stories told because
teasing was what we did, nine years apart, not knowing each
other so well as grown-ups, to show our love even back then
when I was two or three/ That story of the posthole I would
tell on him in answer to his about me throwing my twirling
baton, missing him shattering mother's prized louvered
windows/ and he could counter with the one about me
smoking a Salem menthol behind his bedroom door/I was
in the fourth grade/ *Daddy's gonna catch you and give you*
a whipping/and the time I spray-painted the interior of his
1959 Pontiac our black and gold school colors when he was
away serving in the navy/and later the story of the sound a
spanking makes across a lap on a piano bench, keys tinkling
with each stroke like teeth, a chilled rattle/ These were our
love stories/ but none of our stories could stretch time
enough to stop its thrashing.

Interregnum

I'm no Nemo in Slumberland
hero of that 1904 color comic strip,
a boy swept away in his nightshirt
clinging to a four-poster bed—
his only escape to awake.
Winsor McKay, the artist, animates them—
exotic places, spooky friends, rowdy
adventures—stretching the constricting frames
to hold suppressed desires, terrifying creatures.
Give me instead *The Rarebit Fiend*, McKay's other
masterpiece, with those adult phobias and dark
fantasies where fear itself is repressed
all because of a nibble of cheese and crackers
what I'm sometimes known to eat at bedtime.

I grew up on *Winkin, Blinkin, and Nod*
where fishes were stars and catching them
a slumberers' delight. Such dreams matched
the joys of a '50s childhood with Loretta Young
dolls (such skin!) and authentic Roy Rogers boots.
How then these dreams which tend to blush:
I'm in bed with my band director,
flirt with an old lover who's married,
snap at my mother's hazing (but she was
the sweetest). I watch myself (from a high camera
angle—am I looking down on myself?)
climb walls but never reach the top,
attempt lectures still searching for my notes.
I do dream like you, Nemo—not exactly fantasies,
not exactly nightmares—
a gray fantasmagoria of surprises and misfortunes.
I count them, even that a failed assignment,
all played to a Thelonious Monk jazz tune in my head,
the same dissonant eight bars looping over and over,
like sheep high on melatonin, such dreary leaps.
But then I realize: I am grinding my teeth
(did I forget the night guard?).

I'm tethered in sheets, contemplating Aleve,
blood pressure rising, left hip aching,
snuffled nose caking, torn rotator cuff
waking me. . .

       into an interregnum, that surreal state
between waking and sleeping.

There's only one truth in that nether land,
the flipside of forgotten,
and that's the lines it can yield for a poem.
Through a sinus headache they come crashing down
squeezing the life out of me onto the page.

Poem for John Berger

African, the zoo caretaker said, *the largest*
I had only my plains variety for comparison:
bowling ball small, pinched face, fierce incisors
a conundrum of quills napping in the nearest elm tree.
The sheriff shot him down,
that one, whose nocturnal gnawing
was slowly killing my oldest most treasured tree.
Tree or porcupine, tree or porcupine
 which to save, which to let go?
The thud awakened me as he fell from his perch
suddenly not some distant object easily irradicated
but one who could look back.
Close up he had paddy- cake paws like a child's hands.
And now these—a pair—eating not trees
but grapes and sweet potatoes and dog food,
no foe, no needed defense in this homely zoo.
Their claws grasp breakfast,
They gnaw into tomorrow, quills
a black and white rainbow glistening
no warrior's breastplate, no headdress adorned.
Just quills—sometimes used for writing—
now used by my looking
by my making my story
out of you.

I'm As Old as Turtles (and half as smart)

The pills line up and what a choice:
Solaray's probiotic (Adult 50+)
Curcumin C3 Complex,
Algae Omega, of course, (all those 3's)
Chondroitin by itself (better for the kidney stones),
something called *Golden Revived*
—God knows what—recommended by
a similarly aging friend.

If I took them all at once—these pills—
I might get a glimpse of a holy drug cartel,
of a stoned hereafter.
(Someone once thought I was praying
but it was only scoliosis.)
Instead these pills are staggered throughout the day
like my lurching walk,
my electrified nervy hips,
my bone on bone.

What I really would like,
and over the counter please,
is a tonic for a good fade-away—
jumpshot, that is. Mine best
at the top of the key, floating right,
airborne, flicked wrist away from the fray:
the kind that once stupefied opponents—
all those Friday night basketball games
ago, when the legs were young,
no rotator cuff twinge, no hip bursitis
only the net, nothing but net—
faking out pharmaceuticals and all.
The shot that now exists only
in my melatonin dreams.

Tarantella

No partner but the wind
an intermittent dance of the hours

plants not people ravaged
tree skirts flailing, breezeway wailing

Times past *tarantella* dancers convulsed
swirling to purge a venomous bite

but no relief.

Once at a writing workshop
our leader daily stepped around

beetles, careful not to kill
anything, not even our poems.

I wrote a book about a cartoonist
who drew a strip, *The Worm's Eye View*

so I thought I understood such small wisdom.

And once I played (or tried to play) piano tunes
inspired by that wild cavort

notes missed stirred more frenzy
fingers fanned the hysteria

but no relief.

When the black dot on the door frame
moved, my first thought was *kill it*.

Beetles, scorpions, *ninos de la tierra*
can plague a desert backyard.

Then the tiny dot moved again, a mere
period pulsing in the late day sun

back a brown square—an eighth of an inch,
smaller than your pinkie nail.

I realized too late—and isn't this always the way—
it was a baby tarantula now running, erratic,

over the invisible line of recent pest spray
So tiny! (No large leaper with hooded eyes)

(No migrant blocking country roads)
He dodged and wavered and shuddered.

Perhaps deep down the dancers knew
the bite was no worse than a bee sting

but they persisted, repressed selves
blaming the hairy beast.

Yes, this, too, could be a dance—
that stagger, that lurch (our poison now)

until—not a cry, not a wail—
but a stream of bisque liquid trailed

he was so tiny
he was so tiny

Blue Highway

Is it true that the highway
   fronting our yard
    was a once a dead end?
That the golden cocker named Honey
    nursed her pups in that same
    yard/ kittens too abandoned
    by their mother fleeing boys
    with b b guns
Later, some stranger, when the road had become
    a state highway, peed outside our
    fence /my dad gave chase
Easter photos remind us of that one branched elm
    the one we climbed when not
    posing in our newest spring coats
    our patent leather shoes
The same yard where daddy wrapped a bullwhip
    around my brother who had smarted off
    too many times and not emptied the trash
Where we played basketball on the worn grass
    New Year's Eve/ the parents
    inside listening to Lawrence Welk
    and playing bridge
Where we could hear the peacocks' cries
    from across the street at the Catholic
    church parsonage/ such eerie love
A yard reaching around the house
    bordered by my father's rose garden
a yard that caved in because of an old
    cesspool behind the house
    we wondered if we could
    make a hideout in it
A yard of mixed native grass and intrusive
    Bermuda grasses more water please
Where we could lie on our backs and see the stars
    Or cumulus clouds tease by

Where we fired off plastic rockets loaded
        with baking powder and vinegar, Mother's loss
        Newton's Third Law of Motion
Where a friend and I once held each other
        in a sleeping bag, too late to ring
        the doorbell, home for a holiday
My dad early at his bathroom window
        finally knowing the truth

Eres Tú

after the popular love song of the same name

You, *eres tú*
the swimmer struggling up a clay slick beach
You   who cannot swim
thirst in waters you cannot drink
Desparecida on the border   that
liminal space embraced by cactus thorns
you   taste   a stomach so empty
so brined   in necessary love
And you   the backpack   left by the border wall
hold tight a child's skirt, wrestle discarded bottles
You you   carry a pentimento of loss
You   earth so proud   that you   crack open
sending angry warnings
to the builders blocking monarchs
shaking walls shrouded in barbed wire
You   the soldier who spit when waved
at   reply to our broken Spanish   *puta*
and to you   on the other side of the wall
helicopter a ceaseless tsunami of wind
when you   you   and   you   visited
there   just to see
You   wet cheek   in rivulets running
this rough road through hope and prayers
You   you   *eres tú*
Would I give you the water from my fountain?
the fire from my home?
the bonfire made for sharing?
Eres tú   eres tú
You carry a child wound tight to your breast
through bonfires, bombs, discountenance, starvation
   desesperada   You
cry out to chatting tv hosts
y quien eres tú
And who are you?

To Make a Prairie

Roiled back like a burr
haircut

no wildness in that
conformity, then

ripped and blasted   highways
eviscerate forbs
rise from the dross

once a short grass prairie
by Comanche count teeming
seventy-six medicinal and food plants
they identified

purple prairie clover, amaranth, yarrow,
and those we know: side oats gramma, blue stem,
buffalo gramma, purple ground cherry

beauty
not possessed

 before forgetting before
 cycling droughts of justification

What
disappeared before knowing,

a flickering past,
a buffalo wallow,
listening for a buzz in the grass.

First, the over-grazing   then habitat
loss, no neighbors notice, opting for

widened, improved roads, electrical
towers, the steel will of development.

Never mind the water. Take the
minerals, wind, sun: take take take

There had been yellow headed blackbirds
Lark Buntings blackening fence rows

like the thousands of pigeons exterminated
leaving a vacuous sky

avocets leaped to catch grasshoppers
in that dun sea of grass

Imagine, imagine   that's what's
left

Who am I among the disappeared?
those from Chile, Argentina, Nigeria, the US border

a last Kaua'i'o'o male's solitary song
the presence of absence.

There had been the yearly sightings of western box turtles
toenails clicking as they crossed a caliche road,
what hard pan—a clockwork of seasons.

Tarantulas too, headed west
What we put store by.

 A solitary Swainson hawk
hanging sky, follows the plow

that turns up killdeer and mice
that first turned the prairie

Now atop the tractor we plant the new government mix
We look back over our shoulders

to see where we have been, while
moving forward into our fertilized future.
I did see one Lesser Prairie Chicken in the l990s.
a hen awaiting a male on the booming hill
waiting   waiting
I promise
I did

With Appreciation

Special thanks to friends and writers Zita Arocha and David Smith-Soto for eyes and ears full of listening and encouragement. And to Genneil Curphey for the many exchanged texts of support and sharing. Thank you Darryl Birkenfield for shining a light always on our best selves. To Elizabeth Zarur, dear friend—you inspire with your art. And to Deborah Moore, that inner artist, who always listens.

I am so grateful to teachers, family, and friends who listened, suggested, cared. Special thanks to sage mentor and guide, Juliet Patterson, to BK Loren who believed in the lyric in prose and poetry, and to teachers Joy Harjo and Aimee Nezhukumatathil for your inspiration. And to the Wurlitzer Foundation where this project modestly began and Writing Workshops in Greece where it caught sail.

Shelley Armitage, professor emerita, writer, naturalist, lives in the Chihuahuan desert in Las Cruces, New Mexico. She is author of eight award-winning books, including *John Held, Jr.: Illustrator of the Jazz Age, The World of Rose O'Neill,* and *The Pajarito Journals of Peggy Pond Church. Walking the Llano, A Texas Memoir of Place* was a Kirkus starred book cited as one of the best memoirs of the year, and a finalist for the May Sarton prize, the New Mexico-Arizona book awards, and the Collins P. Carr award from the Texas Institute of Letters. Her first poetry book, *A Habit of Landscape,* won a Spur Award from the Western Writers Association.

Armitage won the Southwest Book Award and the Emily Toth award and was a finalist for the Eudora Welty Prize and the Indies Book of the Year. Her work has been featured on National Public Radio and has appeared in such works as *True Border, Shifting Views and Changing Places: the Photographs of Rick Dingus, Multicultural America, the Southwest Review, The Post-2000 Western, Projecting Words: Writing Images.* Among her honors are a fellowship from the Wurlitzer Foundation, a Distinguished Chair in American Literature Fulbright in Warsaw, Fulbright awards in Finland and Portugal, a National Endowment for the Arts grant, three National Endowment for the Humanities grants, and a Rockefeller grant. She has served on the Swann Foundation at the Library of Congress and as Executive Director of the New Mexico Humanities Council. Her academic appointments include West Texas A&M and the University of Hawai'i at Manoa. She is professor emerita at the University of Texas at El Paso where she held the Roderick Professorship and is a member of the Texas Institute of Letters.

Armitage participates in various conservation practices including New Mexico Site Watch and Tree Stewards. She has been recognized by the US Department of Agriculture for management of her family grasslands near Vega, Texas. There she finds inspiration in how the power of landscape draws us into a greater understanding of ourselves and others as we experience kinship with the places we inhabit.

www.ingramcontent.com/pod-product-compliance
Lightning Source LLC
Chambersburg PA
CBHW022101080426
42734CB00009B/1452